BE FREE IN CHRIST

A Road Map to Freedom for Men

CALEB BRIAN RODGERS

WESTBOW
PRESS®
A DIVISION OF THOMAS NELSON
& ZONDERVAN

WestBow Press books may be ordered through booksellers or by contacting:

WestBow Press
A Division of Thomas Nelson & Zondervan
1663 Liberty Drive
Bloomington, IN 47403
www.westbowpress.com
844-714-3454

Scripture taken from the King James Version of the Bible.

Cover Image Credit: Lexy Wages
Bailey Sherwood and Eddie Strawbridge at Plan House Printing for Graphic Design

ISBN: 978-1-6642-2728-6 (sc)
ISBN: 978-1-6642-2727-9 (e)

Library of Congress Control Number: 2021905021

Print information available on the last page.

WestBow Press rev. date: 04/27/2021

FROM THE AUTHOR

Be sure to let Jesus use my writings to encourage you. More than that, let them bring healing to your soul! Jesus helped me encourage many individuals over these last few years. He's mended many broken hearts and lonely souls. Please read these messages of hope, and enjoy letting Jesus be your one true source of hope. If you make Jesus Lord of your life, you can be free, even in prison!

My deep love for hurting souls has led me to share my past messages tucked away in this devotional journal. May you respond with an open heart!

FROM THE AUTHOR'S PARENTS

Our prayer is that you see a glimpse into our little boy's heart, which is ultimately for everyone to know "his" Jesus and to receive the gift of life and freedom found only in Christ! Jesus is everything to our son, and in his words, "Only eternal things are important!" There would be no greater joy than for one reader to accept Jesus into his or her heart and experience the freedom in Christ that Caleb so desires for everyone!

CONTENTS

TRUST

A message delivered to the men at Transformation Ranch on July 4, 2016.

The Message

Jesus is excited that you all are here. Jesus enjoys everybody, so everybody needs to enjoy Jesus.

Jesus is doing outstanding work, and He needs everyone to trust Him.

One day Jesus is going to need us all to tell our stories so that He can be glorified. Jesus needs us to comfort others the way He comforts us.

Jesus trusts each individual to tell others about Him so that others can one day go to Heaven.

Jesus cares about everyone here, but not everyone here cares about Jesus.

Jesus's desire is for each individual to one day accept Him. But not each individual wants to. Accept Jesus, and He will change your desires.

You have a purpose, though the enemy tries to make you think that you don't. But the Jesus I know tells me that the enemy is not telling the truth. Jesus tells me that each individual has an amazing gift. Only use it to make Jesus happy!

Jesus enjoys everybody listening to me talk about Him.

The Scriptures

> O Lord of hosts, blessed is the man that trusteth in Thee. (Psalm 84:12)

> Return to thine own house, and shew how great things God hath done unto thee. And he went his way, and published throughout the whole city how great things Jesus had done unto him. (Luke 8:39)

> Cast thy burden upon the Lord, and He shall sustain thee: He shall never suffer the righteous to be moved. (Psalm 55:22)

THE REFLECTION

How does life weigh you down?

_____

_____

_____

_____

_____

List two heavy burdens that you can trust God with.

_____

_____

_____

_____

_____

How did this message speak to your heart?

_____

_____

_____

_____

_____

TURN FROM SIN

A message delivered to the men at Transformation Ranch on July 16, 2016.

The Message

Jesus needs everyone to understand that the death of Bryant[1] is going to be used to bring hope to others like him.

The enemy is going to try to destroy other people's lives if everyone doesn't turn to Jesus.

The enemy attacks me because he doesn't want me to tell you that Jesus is the only comfort that we need. Jesus wants me to be sure that everyone here understands that.

Jesus is pleading for each individual here to accept Him, not the enemy.

Jesus loves everyone here!

The Scriptures

> For the wages of sin is death; but the gift of God is eternal life through Jesus Christ our Lord. (Romans 6:23)

> Jesus saith unto him, I am the way, the truth, and the life: no man cometh unto the Father, but by Me. (John 14:6)

> For we wrestle not against flesh and blood, but against principalities, against powers, against the rulers of the darkness of this world, against spiritual wickedness in high places. (Ephesians 6:12)

---

[1] Bryant was a young guy who was in the recovery program during one of Caleb's visits. He passed away from an accident shortly after completing the program.

THE REFLECTION

Let's see if the enemy still deceives you. What sin holds you back from following Jesus?

_____

_____

_____

_____

Please repent of that sin, and follow the One that can set you free. Talk about what things you confessed here.

_____

_____

_____

_____

How did this message speak to your heart?

_____

_____

_____

_____

COMFORT

A message delivered to the men at Transformation Ranch in 2016.

The Message

Jesus needs me to encourage all of you, so that's why I'm here! Jesus has always comforted me, and He will always comfort all of you!

The enemies are trying to discourage you, but don't let them succeed. Jesus tells me that the enemies can't ever defeat Him. Jesus needs everyone here to trust in Him since He is the only one who can be trusted.

Someone from the group said, "Tell us about angels."

"Angels are Jesus's angels. Jesus's angels come to comfort us. Angels are Jesus's heavenly beings. They are always around us. Angels are here today. Angels are always here to comfort us. Jesus enjoys sending His angels to comfort us."

Someone from the group asked, "Have you been able to see Jesus?"

"I've not been able to see Jesus's face, but He has been with me my entire life. He's enough to me. Jesus has helped me through the hardest times in my life. Jesus has always desired me just like He's always desired each individual in this room. Jesus needs each individual in this room to begin to desire His comfort, and He will give that comfort."

Another group member said, "Tell us about Heaven."

"Heaven is beautiful. Heaven is just astounding. Heaven is beyond anything I'm able to describe. In heaven Jesus is always glorified. In Heaven nothing is important except Jesus. In heaven Chloe[2] is there. Jesus is comforting Chloe just like He's comforting Bryant."

Jesus is always fighting for us.

Jesus is beginning to prepare to come for me. Just remember all the things that I've told you each time that I've come. Don't be upset. Just know that Jesus is going to use my death to bring Him glory, just like He's using Bryant's death.

Jesus needs me in heaven for an eternal purpose, even though you[3] and Mommy don't understand yet.

---

[2] Chloe is Caleb's sister, who passed away only six hours after her birth.
[3] Caleb was looking at his daddy when he said, "you."

Jesus is enjoying everyone's attention today. Always talk to Jesus about anything that you need to, and pray for me too.

The Scriptures

> Blessed be God, even the Father of our Lord Jesus Christ, the Father of mercies, and the God of all comfort; who comforteth us in all our tribulation, that we may be able to comfort them which are in any trouble, by the comfort wherewith we ourselves are comforted of God. (2 Corinthians 1:3–4)

> And I will pray the Father, and He shall give you another Comforter, that He may abide with you for ever; Even the Spirit of truth; whom the world cannot receive, because it seeth Him not, neither knoweth Him: but ye know Him; for He dwelleth with you, and shall be in you. I will not leave you comfortless: I will come to you. (John 14:16–18)

> Behold, I send an Angel before thee, to keep thee in the way, and to bring thee into the place which I have prepared. (Exodus 23:20)

THE REFLECTION

Good times come and go, but Jesus never abandons us. Can you give an example of one season when you chose to abandon Jesus?

_____

_____

_____

_____

_____

Please know relishing over bad choices won't make them go away. Repenting of those bad choices and asking to be forgiven will set you free. Take time to write down what you want to be freed from.

_____

_____

_____

_____

How did this message speak to your heart?

_____

_____

_____

_____

ETERNAL THINGS

A message delivered to the men at Transformation Ranch in 2016.

The Message

Jesus is telling me that not every individual understands eternal things. Eternal things are important. Earthly things are not important.

Angels are everywhere, but enemies are too.

Someone from the group asked, "Do angels have wings?"

"Jesus's angels have heavenly appearances but not wings."

Someone from the group asked, "Is the Spirit of God here?"

"Yes."

Another person asked, "What do you see in the atmosphere?"

"I'm seeing enemies telling somebody that it's too difficult to continue being Jesus's servant, so they should be Satan's servant. The angels aren't allowing enemies to destroy that individual."

Please pray that I might tell others about Jesus with my own mouth. I'm just continuing to tell others with Mommy's help until that prayer is answered.

Jesus is enjoying every individual here.

The Scriptures

> Lay not up for yourselves treasures upon Earth, where moth and rust doth corrupt, and where thieves break through and steal: But lay up for yourselves treasures in Heaven, where neither moth nor rust doth corrupt, and where thieves do not break through nor steal. (Matthew 6:19–20)

> But seek ye first the kingdom of God, and His righteousness; and all these things shall be added unto you. (Matthew 6:33)

> Whereas ye know not what shall be on the morrow. For what is your life? It is even a vapour, that appeareth for a little time, and then vanisheth away. (James 4:14)

THE REFLECTION

Planning long bar trips, strip-joint outings, and car raids won't get you eternity in Heaven. Jesus changes those earthly desires into eternal ones. Name two earthly desires that keep you from Jesus.

_____

_____

_____

_____

_____

Holding on to sin causes death. The moment sin entangles them, many individuals fall into Satan's trap. Wouldn't you like to have full assurance that you will have life even after death? Confess all sins and enjoy eternity with Jesus.

_____

_____

_____

_____

_____

How did this message speak to your heart?

_____

_____

_____

_____

TIME WITH JESUS

A message delivered to family in November 2016.

The Message

Jesus desires our time alone with Him, and not just during church. Jesus's time is special. It is beautiful. It's glorious. It's heart-changing.

Eventually, Jesus's time will become all that you desire. Just give it a try. He needs each of us to devote time to Him every day. Enemies don't like the fact that we stop everything to seek Jesus, so be ready for interruptions.

Enemies don't enjoy Christians actually taking time to listen to Jesus. But Christians have to enjoy making the time in order to hear from Jesus. Jesus desires to speak to each person in this room, but it's up to us to hear His voice.

Could each person here devote just ten minutes of quiet time to Jesus? Nothing else, just listening to Him. Don't enjoy telling Him your needs, don't enjoy even thanking Him, don't enjoy talking at all, don't enjoy listening to music, don't enjoy cell phones, don't enjoy family, don't enjoy going to the bathroom, and don't enjoy getting up at all. Just ten minutes each day is all I'm asking. Try it for one week, and tell me what you heard Jesus speak to you.

Now it's important to know enemies aren't going to like this one bit. Enemies are going to do everything in their power to stop this time from occurring. Enemies hate Christians devoting their time to listening to Jesus's voice because that's when miracles happen, that's when things begin to change, that's when enemies get defeated, that's when Christians become the people God created them to be, that's when victories occur, that's when battles are conquered, that's when mountains move.

So is everyone in? Amen!

The Scriptures

> And the apostles gathered themselves together unto Jesus, and told Him all things, both what they had done, and what they had taught. And He said unto them, Come ye yourselves apart into a desert place, and rest a while: for there were many coming and going, and they had no leisure so much as to eat. (Mark 6:30–31)

> Be still, and know that I am God: I will be exalted among the heathen, I will be exalted in the earth. (Psalm 46:10)

No man can serve two masters: for either he will hate the one, and love the other; or else he will hold to the one, and despise the other. Ye cannot serve God and mammon. Therefore I say unto you, Take no thought for your life, what ye shall eat, or what ye shall drink; nor yet for your body, what ye shall put on. Is not the life more than meat, and the body than raiment? Behold the fowls of the air: for they sow not, neither do they reap, nor gather into barns; yet your heavenly Father feedeth them. Are ye not much better than they? Which of you by taking thought can add one cubit unto his stature? And why take ye thought for raiment? Consider the lilies of the field, how they grow; they toil not, neither do they spin: And yet I say unto you, That even Solomon in all his glory was not arrayed like one of these. Wherefore, if God so clothe the grass of the field, which to day is, and to morrow is cast into the oven, shall He not much more clothe you, O ye of little faith? Therefore take no thought, saying, What shall we eat? or, What shall we drink? or, Wherewithal shall we be clothed? (For after all these things do the Gentiles seek:) for your heavenly Father knoweth that ye have need of all these things. But seek ye first the kingdom of God, and His righteousness; and all these things shall be added unto you. Take therefore no thought for the morrow: for the morrow shall take thought for the things of itself. Sufficient unto the day is the evil thereof. (Matthew 6:24–34)

THE REFLECTION

Being still before Jesus requires time. Lots of time is given to each of us every day. Compile a list of everything that gets your time in one day. How much time does Jesus get?

_____

_____

_____

_____

Start today by being quiet for one minute alone with Jesus. Try not to talk, only listen. Concentrate on the name of Jesus. Do this each day, adding one minute each time until you can still your body for ten minutes. Keep a journal about how Jesus teaches children to rest with Him.

_____

_____

_____

_____

How did this message speak to your heart?

_____

_____

_____

_____

JESUS'S COMFORT

A message delivered on Faith Ministries TV Broadcasting Station, December 2016, with Mr. Bob McCustion.

The Message

Jesus is using me to help others understand that He is truly all that we need. Hearts are being broken each day by the enemies, and Jesus is the only One who can mend those broken hearts. Mr. Bob, Christians often don't turn to Jesus's comfort like they should. Christians turn to other things instead of His comfort. It's hard to understand their thinking. Couldn't we try to help other Christians realize that Jesus's comfort is all they need? I'll be glad to help you tell them.

I'm living proof since it's terrible to be trapped in this body that doesn't do what I want it to do. But Jesus's comfort is always enough. It's easy for me because Jesus continually meets my needs. My mommy and daddy teach me to depend on Jesus, not anything else, Mr. Bob. Healing isn't important to me, but Jesus's continuous comfort is. It's not my desire to be able to enjoy earthly things, but it is my desire to enjoy eternal things. Jesus's desires are my desires. Other individuals might think I'm only just saying that, but I'm serious when I talk about Jesus.

The Scriptures

> My hands also will I lift up unto Thy commandments, which I have loved; and I will meditate in Thy statutes. Remember the word unto Thy servant, upon which Thou hast caused me to hope. This is my comfort in my affliction: for Thy word hath quickened me. (Psalm 119:48–50)

> The Lord also will be a refuge for the oppressed, a refuge in times of trouble. (Psalm 9:9)

> One thing have I desired of the Lord, that will I seek after; that I may dwell in the house of the Lord all the days of my life, to behold the beauty of the Lord, and to inquire in His temple. For in the time of trouble He shall hide me in His pavilion: in the secret of His tabernacle shall He hide me; He shall set me up upon a rock. (Psalm 27:4–5)

THE REFLECTION

Being confined to eternity in hell could easily be your sentence for your sins. Hear me tell you that Jesus longs for you to be confined with Him! He's already paid for your pardon from hell. He longs for you to turn to Him. Would you count on Jesus to comfort you right where you are? Sit with Jesus, and write how this settles your soul.

_____

_____

_____

_____

List ten things that comfort you in difficult situations. How many of those things guarantee you lasting comfort? Make Jesus number one on your list, and that will be the only list you need.

_____

_____

_____

_____

How did this message speak to your heart?

_____

_____

_____

_____

_____

GOD'S GRACE

A message delivered to the men at Transformation Ranch on January 21, 2017.

The Message

It's been so long since my last visit. Everyone here is special to Jesus. Hasn't Jesus been so good to us. Let us join together and sing "Amazing Grace." Amen.

Aren't your souls at peace as you sing that song? Amazing grace! Amazing grace! Amazing grace! Amazing grace! Haven't each of us been recipients of God's amazing grace? Not all of you here have fully understood God's grace, so let me help you.

Grace is for everyone. All you need to do is to be ready to enjoy God's grace. God's grace doesn't cost anything, and it's always available. God's grace is for haters, solitary men, murderers, problem-starters, hotheads, liars, bullies, for all of us. It costs you nothing, but it cost Jesus everything.

My Jesus died a terrible death for every individual in this place. Couldn't you just accept His grace? Couldn't you just accept His love for you? Couldn't you just understand that Jesus isn't a fairy tale? Jesus is real. Jesus is real!

Jesus is everything to me. Jesus is enough of everything to me. He comforts me each minute of the day. There is a reason I'm here tonight. It's for someone in this room who thinks God's grace isn't for them. That's just Satan deceiving you. God's grace is more than enough to cover all your sins, all your lonely nights, all your heartaches, all your failures, all your guilt, all your mistakes, all your childhood hurtful memories, all your weary souls, all of your everything!

Please let me be clear. God's grace is favor that you don't deserve. But it's favor God chooses to have on your life anyway. Couldn't you just accept this and allow God's grace to come into your hearts and enjoy never questioning God's grace again?

Enjoy His grace!

The Scriptures

> For the grace of God that bringeth salvation hath appeared to all men, Teaching us that, denying ungodliness and worldly lusts, we should live soberly, righteously, and godly, in this present world; (Titus 2:11–12)

And He said unto me, My grace is sufficient for thee: for My strength is made perfect in weakness. Most gladly therefore will I rather glory in my infirmities, that the power of Christ may rest upon me. (2 Corinthians 12:9)

For by grace are ye saved through faith; and that not of yourselves: it is the gift of God: Not of works, lest any man should boast. (Ephesians 2:8–9)

THE REFLECTION

How can defiant individuals be deserving of God's grace? The answer is they acknowledge their bad actions and confess their sins to God. God then chooses to forgive their mistakes at that moment. That is grace. Jesus paid the price for grace to be free. Search your heart now. Do you need God's grace?

_____

_____

_____

_____

Being forgiven allows you to move on with hope. Grace allows you a new beginning. Is there someone you need to forgive?

_____

_____

_____

_____

How did this message speak to your heart?

_____

_____

_____

_____

SUFFERING

A message delivered to the men at Transformation Ranch on September 2, 2017.

The Message

My name is Caleb. But you can call me Preacher.

Enemies have tried to keep me from being here for months now, but I'm finally here to deliver God's words for you.

Can we join together and sing "Amazing Grace"? You lead us.

I'm going to share with you my song.*[4]

Amazing Grace. How sweet the sound that saved a wretch like me.

Feeling happy each day is truly hard, but God enjoys helping us through difficult days.

Enemies constantly come against me because Jesus is my everything. Mommy's always battling the enemies because she loves Jesus so much and is attacked constantly, but our family is not going to stop serving Jesus. It's frustrating to suffer for Christ, but He did the most suffering for us on the cross. Ask yourself if Jesus is worth everything to you, or do you prefer to have an easy life? Always know Jesus cares so much about everyone in this room. Even the worst of sinners here. And enemies would like to see you dead, not alive.

The Scriptures

> Plead my cause, O Lord, with them that strive with me: fight against them that fight against me. (Psalm 35:1)

> Let us therefore come boldly unto the throne of grace, that we may obtain mercy, and find grace to help in time of need. (Hebrews 4:16)

> I came not to call the righteous, but sinners to repentance. (Luke 5:32)

---

[4] Caleb's revised version of "Amazing Grace" can be found on page 52.

THE REFLECTION

Being under constant persecution can cause the best believers to halt doing the Lord's commandments, me included. Called to continue past our suffering are we all. Face it, child of God, you're not in the war to turn on Christ. Christ desires to use your pain to turn others to Him. Please ask God to allow your pain and suffering to minister to others.

_____

_____

_____

_____

Give yourself time to mourn for whatever you feel has hurt you. Write about that. When the time is right, allow God to use the hurt for good.

_____

_____

_____

_____

How did this message speak to your heart?

_____

_____

_____

_____

BATTLES

A message delivered on October 8, 2017.

The Message

Turning your eyes away from our families and turning your eyes only to Jesus's message is my desire tonight. Just understand you're important to us, and our ultimate hope is for someone to run to Jesus's arms tonight.

Enemies surround us on all sides, but you need not be concerned. Jesus fights your battles and my battles and mommy's battles and daddy's battles. Hold on to Jesus with everything you have. Don't give up hope. Only trust that Jesus truly is everything you need.

Lately Mommy hasn't been up to herself because enemies have been trying to stop her from telling others to put their trust in Jesus. But she's stronger than the enemies because God is her strength.

Always talk to God about your struggles; He will listen. Finally, stay close to Jesus, and you won't be defeated.

The Scriptures

> For He shall give His angels charge over thee, to keep thee in all thy ways. (Psalm 91:11)

> Trust in the Lord with all thine heart; and lean not unto thine own understanding. In all thy ways acknowledge Him, and He shall direct thy paths. (Proverbs 3:5–6)

> Why art thou cast down, O my soul? and why art thou disquieted within me? hope thou in God: for I shall yet praise Him, who is the health of my countenance, and my God. (Psalm 42:11)

THE REFLECTION

Healing comes from God alone. My battles and your battles move us either against or closer to letting Jesus heal what appears to be attacking us. God understands people are hesitant to ask for His help because they're afraid to admit their weaknesses. I am the first to admit I battle with letting big kids near me because they don't understand cerebral palsy. They only understand I'm able to do things with my parents' help. I'm always depending on others for everything, but I choose to trust Jesus to heal me and battle for me. How can you relate? What situations do you need to let Jesus take over?

_____

_____

_____

_____

Hard days seem to move most people away from God, but He desires each person to lean on Him even more when days are especially difficult. Can you give five circumstances over to God, completely trusting that He can turn them into good? What circumstances did you choose?

_____

_____

_____

_____

How did this message speak to your heart?

_____

_____

_____

_____

FORGIVENESS

A message delivered to the men at Broken Lives on December 12, 2017.

The Message

Lots of guilt appears to be here. Forgive yourselves because God forgives you! Contrary to what you feel, you are forgiven!

Lately believers really seem frustrated at themselves. But God desires His children to lose their frustration and begin to see themselves through His eyes. Blaming yourself for turning away from God's path and following the enemy always leads to much guilt. Kindly let God remove your guilt. Put away your old self, and allow God to free you!

Seek ye first the kingdom of God, not the kingdom of your flesh!

The Scriptures

> I acknowledged my sin unto Thee, and mine iniquity have I not hid. I said, I will confess my transgressions unto the Lord; and Thou forgavest the iniquity of my sin. Selah. (Psalm 32:5)

> There is therefore now no condemnation to them which are in Christ Jesus, who walk not after the flesh, but after the Spirit. (Romans 8:1)

> Therefore if any man be in Christ, he is a new creature: old things are passed away; behold, all things are become new. (2 Corinthians 5:17)

THE REFLECTION

Following Christ comes easily for me because He constantly comforts me and delights in our time together. Each day begins with me thanking Jesus for loving me enough to die for my sins. Then I enjoy asking Jesus to forgive me of my many mistakes, especially when I complain about Mother's healthy cooking. Jesus allows me to talk to Him about anything. Is there something you need to ask Jesus to enjoy forgiving?

_____

_____

_____

_____

_____

Hear me loud and clear: Jesus forgives you! Tell Jesus about it, and enjoy thanking Him for His forgiveness that frees you to forgive.

_____

_____

_____

_____

_____

How did this message speak to your heart?

_____

_____

_____

_____

_____

BODIES BROKEN FOR CHRIST

A message delivered to the men at Broken Lives on January 15, 2018.

The Message

Broken are all of us, but Jesus's blood binds our broken lives in order for all of us to heal! Go enjoy calling on Jesus's safety net today in your moment of desperate need. He paves the way before us and teaches us to make the best decisions. Praying to God helps you to find fulfillment, but beating up on yourself about the bad decisions you've made only leads to destruction. Continuous destruction leads to death.

Hear Mommy's voice loud enough to hear what I am yelling out from God! Be transformed this morning by the renewal of your minds! Hell isn't a fairy tale; it's a terribly evil burning fire that doesn't stop burning. Forget the bad choices you've made, and enjoy asking God to forgive you. Then go and sin no more!

The Scriptures

> The Spirit of the Lord God is upon me; because the Lord hath anointed me to preach good tidings unto the meek; He hath sent me to bind up the brokenhearted, to proclaim liberty to the captives, and the opening of the prison to them that are bound; (Isaiah 61:1)

> And be not conformed to this world: but be ye transformed by the renewing of your mind, that ye may prove what is that good, and acceptable, and perfect, will of God. (Romans 12:2)

> When Jesus had lifted up Himself, and saw none but the woman, He said unto her, Woman, where are those thine accusers? hath no man condemned thee? She said, No man, Lord. And Jesus said unto her, Neither do I condemn thee: go, and sin no more. (John 8:10–11)

THE REFLECTION

Holding clocks in front of our faces doesn't cause time to hurry up or slow down. We have no control over time; but we do have control over how we use our time. Stop wasting time reliving past mistakes. Give God control over your mind, and He will remind you that He doesn't bring up mistakes He's already forgiven. Today, tell the enemy God loves you. What else can you hear God tell you?

_____

_____

_____

_____

_____

List five lies Satan whispers to you. Replace those lies with what God says about His most cherished child.

_____

_____

_____

_____

_____

How did this message speak to your heart?

_____

_____

_____

_____

_____

COMMIT TO GOD

A message delivered to the men at Transformation Ranch on January 20, 2018.

The Message

Are you all believing that you are forgiven?

Are you all believing forgiveness comes from God?

A young boy am I, but God enjoys forgiving me when I truly ask Him to, and you're older than me. Think about that. You asking God's forgiveness is no different if you truly repent.

Am I appointed to be here for someone in this room? I think so. Am I struggling with enemies daily? I think so. Remember all of us battle enemies constantly, but God is always fighting for us.

Allow me to put you in my shoes. Mommy helps me urinate in the morning. Then I depend on her for absolutely every need I have all day long. All I'm able to do is trust Mommy to feed me, clothe me, make sure I don't urinate on myself, teach me to believe God's teachings, enjoy staying close to me for constant comfort, and all my other needs. If my mommy is committed to me, don't you think God is even more committed to each of you.

The Scriptures

> Ye shall not fear them: for the Lord your God He shall fight for you. (Deuteronomy 3:22)

> Repent ye therefore, and be converted, that your sins may be blotted out, when the times of refreshing shall come from the presence of the Lord; (Acts 3:19)

> To open their eyes, and to turn them from darkness to light, and from the power of Satan unto God, that they may receive forgiveness of sins, and inheritance among them which are sanctified by faith that is in Me. (Acts 26:18)

THE REFLECTION

Battles are constant for many of us. Getting flat on our faces is how we fight our battles. Gaining victory comes when we allow God control over each circumstance. List the biggest challenge ahead of you. Ask God to battle for you.

_____

_____

_____

_____

_____

People fail at admitting their weaknesses. Part of the reason is pride. God delights in His children when they humble themselves, ask for forgiveness, and commit themselves to surrendering to what God has. Pride keeps many people from living fully committed to God. Must you hold on to pride? Continued hotheadedness isn't a sign of someone who has humbled himself. Name one area of your life you're refusing to give to God. Ask God to forgive you, and enjoy giving God control.

_____

_____

_____

_____

How did this message speak to your heart?

_____

_____

_____

_____

_____

CONTENTMENT

A message during some of the most painful times endured in the summer of 2018.

The Message

Years of tough trials have utterly taught me to be content in all things. Time and time again, I've asked God to heal me. Time and time again, God chooses not to enjoy answering my petitions to Him. He's choosing instead to comfort me in order that I might comfort those with the comfort God freely gives to me!

Punishing me He is not! Preparing me He is!

Facing pain nearly every day hasn't been enjoyable for me. But going through the pain has made me who God desires me to be. A painful burden has been placed on me, but navigating my pain to gain people for Christ transforms the burden into a blessing.

Preacher is my other name. Preaching God's teachings is my assignment. Hard times do come, but my God's Word tells me He won't leave me.

Most understand what it's like to hurt, but most don't understand what it's like to trust Jesus to replace the hurt with joy! People hurt over most anything, but hurt doesn't have to mean that joy isn't present. Happiness is a feeling brought on after a painful episode has taken huge steps away from baffling looks of others who can't explain such terrible pain. Praises go up after bearing hundreds of bad, painful, intense electrical shocks needed hourly to help others understand God uses hundreds of shocks geared for pain for us to put our faith in Him![5] Pain pulls good people toward taking their own lives if God is a tap of water instead of a glass of living water in painful times of their lives.

The Scriptures

> Not that I speak in respect of want: for I have learned, in whatsoever state I am, therewith to be content. I know both how to be abased, and I know how to abound: every where and in all things I am instructed both to be full and to be hungry, both to abound and to suffer need. I can do all things through Christ which strengtheneth me. (Philippians 4:11–13)

> Now the God of hope fill you with all joy and peace in believing, that ye may abound in hope, through the power of the Holy Ghost. (Romans 15:13)

---

[5] The electrical shocks refers to some extremely painful burning episodes in his head that kept him homebound for weeks at a time in the past.

Wherefore seeing we also are compassed about with so great a cloud of witnesses, let us lay aside every weight, and the sin which doth so easily beset us, and let us run with patience the race that is set before us, Looking unto Jesus the author and finisher of our faith; who for the joy that was set before Him endured the cross, despising the shame, and is set down at the right hand of the throne of God. For consider Him that endured such contradiction of sinners against Himself, lest ye be wearied and faint in your minds. (Hebrews 12:1–3)

THE REFLECTION

Great pain continues to be bringing me closer to Jesus. I get better for a few days before pain levels begin to increase again. I could choose to blame God, but I choose to praise Him instead. What are you blaming God for? What pain keeps you from praising God?

_____

_____

_____

_____

_____

Make a conscious choice to remove the blame from God. Make a conscious choice to remember how much God loves you. Punish God no longer with blame. Today start praising God when tough situations arise. Praise God in the bad and the good. Write one thing you can praise God for.

_____

_____

_____

_____

How did this message speak to your heart?

_____

_____

_____

_____

PAINFUL TIMES

A message delivered to the men at Broken Lives on July 27, 2018.

The Message

Battles are painful!

Pain teaches us to enjoy approaching God after all attempts have failed.

Battles are fought alone at times!

Peace in place of pain gets us past our circumstances.

Broken lives aren't broken any longer after Jesus makes that path pain-free. Pain-free doesn't mean hurt doesn't come.

It means we don't have to be hurting without hope! Pain-free favors praising God during pain and peace.

Forget making pain disappear; enjoy making Jesus your partner in the pain!

The Scriptures

> For Thou hast girded me with strength unto the battle: Thou hast subdued under me those that rose up against me. (Psalm 18:39)

> Now the Lord of peace Himself give you peace always by all means. The Lord be with you all. (2 Thessalonians 3:16)

> And all this assembly shall know that the Lord saveth not with sword and spear: for the battle is the Lord's, and He will give you into our hands. (1 Samuel 17:47)

THE REFLECTION

Getting up each morning and gaining strength for another day in pain doesn't happen without God's help. How tough the days could be trying to battle pain in my own strength. How do you get through each day?

_____

_____

_____

_____

Sand on seashores make up black beaches in some parts of the earth. Those beaches aren't any less important than other beaches. We struggle with many different things, and each struggle is important to God. Could you enjoy telling God your struggles by writing Him a letter? Plan on reading it aloud to Him, and plan on thanking Him for using the problems to grow your faith.

_____

_____

_____

_____

How did this message speak to your heart?

_____

_____

_____

_____

_____

COMPLETE FREEDOM

A message delivered to the men at Transformation Ranch at Tombigbee State Park Retreat on August 10, 2018.

The Message

Could you enjoy clinging constantly to Jesus?

Bad choices have been made in the past by most of us. Jesus forgives you, but not everyone else chooses to. Forgive yourselves! Don't be concerned if others don't. Jesus loves you! Enjoy being concerned about that.

Bond yourselves to Jesus! A life bonded to Jesus is a life Jesus can use. There are people who continue to bond with the enemy, and the enemy will use you to take your life. Cease clinging to the enemy now, before it's too late. Feels like some don't believe Jesus is enough.

Put yourselves in my body only for a minute. Pain keeps me confined inside my home most of the time. Ask yourselves how you could be me. Jesus fills my cup daily. Pain stops me from doing many things, but Jesus covers me in His love, and that is more than enough. Pain may keep me bound, but Jesus frees me.

Wouldn't you like to be free? Free from all your pain and free from being bound to the enemy. Jesus is the answer. He loves all of you, regardless of your past. Please come to know my Jesus.

The Scriptures

> Rejoice the soul of Thy servant: for unto Thee, O Lord, do I lift up my soul. For Thou, Lord, art good, and ready to forgive; and plenteous in mercy unto all them that call upon Thee. (Psalm 86:4–5)

> Thou preparest a table before me in the presence of mine enemies: Thou anointest my head with oil; my cup runneth over. Surely goodness and mercy shall follow me all the days of my life: and I will dwell in the house of the Lord for ever. (Psalm 23:5–6)

> Stand fast therefore in the liberty wherewith Christ hath made us free, and be not entangled again with the yoke of bondage. (Galatians 5:1)

THE REFLECTION

Getting set free from pain may be part of God's plans for me, or it may not. Being freed from my sins is no doubt God's plan. Must enemies make you doubt you can be forgiven and set free by true repentance? Make it a priority to ask God for His forgiveness. Please use this space for talking to God.

_____

_____

_____

_____

_____

Many Christians have to choose between calling prison a burden or calling it a blessing. Prison can be anywhere God has placed you for a time. It may be one day or for a lifetime. God uses that time to grow your trust in Him. People often view these times as punishment, but they're really blessings. How do you view your sentence? Enjoy asking God for faith to begin to see prison as a blessing.

_____

_____

_____

_____

How did this message speak to your heart?

_____

_____

_____

_____

_____

BROKEN

A message delivered to the Transformation Home on September 15, 2018.

The Message

Fall is on the way, but a tough summer it's been for me. Have any women/men here experienced tough summers?

Painful summers teach us to go deeper in our walks. Painful summers will work on your mind if you allow them to, but painful agony calls us to let God change our focus.

Some of you have been on a painful walk. Forgive yourselves for any pain brought on by you. God has already forgiven you. Broken women and men are here, and my God allows us to be broken right to the end, sometimes for us to surrender our lives to Him.

Being broken for God isn't bad. Being broken for God puts us in a place where we can be used. God can use broken women and men. Always remember you are God's child. God enjoys piecing His children back together.

Mother has stuck by my bedside at my most broken moments. God desires to stick close at your side. Pain will not overtake me because God fights for me, and God fights for you. Pain will not finish me off because God has a plan for me, and He has a plan for all of you.

Please fight through all the lies until the truth is found. Please brave the storms until Jesus is found. Please make it through this program, and then God promises to walk you through it.

The Scriptures

> Though He slay me, yet will I trust in Him: (Job 13:15)

> When thou passest through the waters, I will be with thee; and through the rivers, they shall not overflow thee: when thou walkest through the fire, thou shalt not be burned; neither shall the flame kindle upon thee. (Isaiah 43:2)

> God is our refuge and strength, a very present help in trouble. (Psalm 46:1)

THE REFLECTION

Count it joy, the hurt, the chaos, the lies, the madness, the loneliness, the burnt bridges, and the charges against you. Make plans to leave painful memories in the past. Make a list of blessings you can praise God for. Ask God to help you focus on blessings instead of painful memories.

_____

_____

_____

_____

_____

How can brokenness help draw each of us closer to Jesus? Think about how tough moments create opportunities to cling to Jesus. He enjoys when we draw near to Him in each circumstance. Recall a time when Jesus comforted you in a broken moment.

_____

_____

_____

_____

_____

How did this message speak to your heart?

_____

_____

_____

_____

_____

ALONE

A message delivered to the men at Transformation Ranch on December 8, 2018.

The Message

Healing is taking place here! Courts may rule against you, but Jesus is on your side. Let's unite and remember what Christmas means.

Many of you will be alone this Christmas, alone from your loved ones. But if you have Jesus Christ, then you're never alone. Christmas isn't about trees, buying expensive gifts, lights, a bunch of parties, Santa, reindeer. Christmas is about remembering God's greatest gift to this earth. Jesus Christ is that gift. The greatest gift any of us could receive because Jesus is enough of everything.

Guys, life is full of suffering. Guys, I suffer through each day just to be alive. Jesus has taught me about suffering for His glory. Painful days I go through when Mother has to do everything for me. Hear me out. It's not easy on her, but I am trusting that one day God is going to heal me.

Follow me as I tell you a story.

A great drought came over the earth. No water was anywhere in sight. People everywhere were dying.

A baby was born in Bethlehem. Finally people would have hope.

Jesus gave people living water, and lives were forever changed.

Must you wait until people approach you to accept Jesus's living water?

I can lead you to the well. Suffer alone no more, guys. Why do you wait? Do you enjoy being alone? He stands at the door. Leave your hurts in the past. You are forgiven.

Make tonight the night when my Jesus becomes yours. Thirst no more.

Rear your children to know and love God. Amen. It will make the earth better.

The Scriptures

> For God so loved the world, that He gave His only begotten Son, that whosoever believeth in Him should not perish, but have everlasting life. (John 3:16)

For I reckon that the sufferings of this present time are not worthy to be compared with the glory which shall be revealed in us. (Romans 8:18)

There cometh a woman of Samaria to draw water: Jesus saith unto her, Give me to drink. (For His disciples were gone away unto the city to buy meat.) Then saith the woman of Samaria unto Him, How is it that Thou, being a Jew, askest drink of me, which am a woman of Samaria? for the Jews have no dealings with the Samaritans. Jesus answered and said unto her, If thou knewest the gift of God, and who it is that saith to thee, Give me to drink; thou wouldest have asked of Him, and He would have given thee living water. The woman saith unto Him, Sir, Thou hast nothing to draw with, and the well is deep: from whence then hast Thou that living water? Art Thou greater than our father Jacob, which gave us the well, and drank thereof himself, and his children, and his cattle? Jesus answered and said unto her, Whosoever drinketh of this water shall thirst again: But whosoever drinketh of the water that I shall give him shall never thirst; but the water that I shall give him shall be in him a well of water springing up into everlasting life. (John 4:7–14)

THE REFLECTION

Please remember you are never alone. Weeks of isolation tend to feel utterly lonely, but Jesus is always with us. Please get your mind off of feeling lonely, and focus on how you can stay encouraged. Someone else needs to be encouraged by you! What could you do today to encourage one individual?

_____

_____

_____

_____

Could I deem each one of you taken? You may think nobody even knows you exist. Jesus assures us that He's near to the brokenhearted. You're His treasure! Cease thinking any differently. Read in Mark chapter 3 about being accepted. Create a handy notebook to write down truths about who Jesus comforts. Enjoy remembering you are on His list.

_____

_____

_____

_____

How did this message speak to your heart?

_____

_____

_____

_____

_____

HOLD ON TO JESUS

A message delivered to the men at Transformation Ranch on February 23, 2019.

The Message

Each time I come here begins a new journey for someone. Abilities are in this room.

People often call cerebral palsy a disability, but I call it just a label. Cerebral palsy becomes a disability if I allow my bad days power in my mind. Cerebral palsy doesn't define me. God defines me.

About labels. Many of you here have been labeled, bad husband, bad father. Feels bad being labeled. People can place labels on us all day long, but God labels us chosen! Clean out thinking any less of yourself than who God says you are. Please ask me if you need to be reminded. Don't ask the world because they don't know you the way God knows you. The world isn't for you, but God is.

Has anyone here been on the verge of suicide? If you have, I'm here tonight for you because you are being deceived. Battles are raging inside your minds but game on for God! Game on because God already knows Pastor Caleb needed to be here tonight. Suicide is for people who have no hope. But I am here tonight on behalf of Jesus Christ because Jesus is our hope. Amen!

After I return home and gather more distance from you, enemies will begin to attack some of your minds. Hold on to what I said about Jesus being our hope.

The Scriptures

> For though we walk in the flesh, we do not war after the flesh: (For the weapons of our warfare are not carnal, but mighty though God to the pulling down of strong holds;) Casting down imaginations, and every high thing that exalteth itself against the knowledge of God, and bringing into captivity every thought to the obedience of Christ; (2 Corinthians 10:3–5)

> Submit yourselves therefore to God. Resist the devil, and he will flee from you. (James 4:7)

> For to be carnally minded is death; but to be spiritually minded is life and peace. (Romans 8:6)

THE REFLECTION

Coaches aren't called coaches because their earthly fathers gave them that name. Coaches acquired their label by helping others succeed. Coaches could cure cancer, but others would most likely continue to label them coaches instead of doctors. No matter what we do, our God-given label is "chosen." How do others label you? How do you label yourself?

_____

_____

_____

_____

_____

Models may be heading down walkways seemingly happy to be labeled beautiful, but they may label themselves dirty. It's not important how we busy ourselves putting labels on each other, but it's critically important to know how God labels each of us! Brother, write the following, I am chosen!

_____

_____

_____

_____

How did this message speak to your heart?

_____

_____

_____

_____

_____

PEACE

A message delivered to the men at Transformation Ranch on March 23, 2019.

The Message

Peaceful and comforting it is at this moment. Guys, believe me, remember this moment.

Cling to thoughts of peace because chaos and turmoil are everywhere. Moments of peace should be treasured. God tells us we can constantly have peace in our minds. Enemies love to fill our minds with garbage. Praising God instead of focusing on the garbage brings about peace. People tend to think they get peace by turning to others for answers, but God has all the answers.

The Scriptures

> And the peace of God, which passeth all understanding, shall keep your hearts and minds through Christ Jesus. (Philippians 4:7)

> Finally, brethren, whatsoever things are true, whatsoever things are honest, whatsoever things are just, whatsoever things are pure, whatsoever things are lovely, whatsoever things are of good report; if there be any virtue, and if there be any praise, think on these things. (Philippians 4:8)

> Take therefore no thought for the morrow: for the morrow shall take thought for the things of itself. Sufficient unto the day is the evil thereof. (Matthew 6:34)

THE REFLECTION

Ballet appears to be a peaceful art. Basketball appears chaotic. Pages of fabulous books are written behind closed doors without the distractions of this world. Fabulous books are also written among many distractions. Ballet, basketball, and writing fabulous books have all gained many happy supporters desiring to be involved because of only seeing the result of commitment. During the peaceful and chaotic moments, God used both to create something others could enjoy. Do not let others convince you that hectic and chaotic moments can't be used to lead others to Christ. Has there been a past experience when peace seemed gone?

_____

_____

_____

_____

Flee from bringing chaos of the past into the peace of the present. Run from things that constantly steal your peace. Make a list of thoughts that give you peace. Tell Jesus to bring those things to mind when you're undergoing chaotic moments and He will.

_____

_____

_____

_____

How did this message speak to your heart?

_____

_____

_____

_____

ANXIETY

A message delivered to the men from Transformation Ranch in our home on May 4, 2019.

The Message

I am glad people here enjoy praising God.

Galatians discusses the fruits of the Spirit, and being held captive to anxiety and worry aren't good fruits. Anxiety leaves many of us praying and worrying at the same time. Prayer pleases God. Anxiety does not. Lately, healing is far from my burden to carry. Anxious thoughts about not being healed no longer control me. Carrying the pain of cerebral palsy no longer burdens me. God healed me from being attacked daily at the thought of having to endure pain daily, never healed. I am at peace because God is using all my challenges for His glory.

Challenges for many of you are not pain and cerebral palsy but anxiety and worry. Being able to finally give God control and know His plans are for me have made all the difference. Please believe me. Facing each day isn't easy for me, but God needs me to know He is doing a beautiful work. And He needs me to depend on Him daily (Matthew 19:13).

The Scriptures

> But the fruit of the Spirit is love, joy, peace, longsuffering, gentleness, goodness, faith, Meekness, temperance: against such there is no law. (Galatians 5:22–23)

> Be careful (anxious) for nothing; but in every thing by prayer and supplication with thanksgiving let your requests be made known unto God. And the peace of God, which passeth all understanding, shall keep your hearts and minds through Christ Jesus. (Philippians 4:6–7)

> I will lift up mine eyes unto the hills, from whench cometh my help. My help cometh from the Lord, which made Heaven and Earth. (Psalm 121:1–2)

THE REFLECTION

Being anxious puts weight on us that God would rather carry. Pages of books have been published about anxiety. Pages of the Bible have been penned about anxiety as well. God's Word has all the answers we need. Would you take some time and allow God to gently replace anxiety with peace by reading His words?

_____

_____

_____

_____

_____

Please bind up constant thoughts of failing others. Thoughts should be about allowing God to use your mistakes to encourage others. Freedom isn't free. Jesus paid the ultimate price for each of us to be free. He didn't suffer for us to remain in bondage to anxiety. Men, I encourage each of you to make a list of anxious thoughts that you can surrender to God today.

_____

_____

_____

_____

How did this message speak to your heart?

_____

_____

_____

_____

_____

BELIEVE

A message delivered to the men at Transformation Ranch on October 2019.

The Message

Can I enjoy about ten minutes of your time tonight? Jesus certainly enjoys each of His children. No exception!

Being here isn't an accident for any of you. God delights in all of you. Don't believe the enemy if you think otherwise. Cease giving that another thought.

Believe God forgives. Believe God comforts. Believe God cares. Believe God. Believe God. Believe God. If you believe something else, then you believe the enemy.

Hard times have caused you to doubt, to doubt that our God is trustworthy. I'm here tonight to enjoy telling you all that, especially in the hard times, God can be trusted. I have endured much difficulty in my short life. Jesus took my difficult situation and used it to help others that struggle. Maybe I've never smuggled drugs. Maybe I've never beat my wife. Maybe I've never thought about murder. But I'm in need of constant rescuing, just like you. Jesus, He is the answer.

Jesus! Turn your life over to Jesus. There will still be difficulties. Trust me! But I don't endure them alone. You can know Him tonight if you desire. It is quite simple really. Jesus. Ask Him to help you and to forgive your sins. Ask Him into your heart. And then enjoy being certain you're a child of God. No enemy can take that from you!

The Scriptures

> Thou shalt no more be termed Forsaken; neither shall thy land any more be termed Desolate: but thou shalt be called Hephzibah, and thy land Beulah: for the Lord delighteth in thee, and thy land shall be married. (Isaiah 62:4)

> But as many as received Him, to them gave He power to become the sons of God, even to them that believe on His name: (John 1:12)

> And he believed in the Lord; and He counted it to him for righteousness. (Genesis 15:6)

THE REFLECTION

Hundreds of thousands of individuals choose to believe the enemies over the one true God. Honestly, build your future on knowing God's truth because Satan constantly feeds us lies. What truth is God telling you today, and what lie do you need not believe?

_____

_____

_____

_____

Many times enemies lead us to think we aren't worthy to even live. Stop believing those terrible lies. Memorize Psalm 112:10. Enemies have no authority over the true God.

_____

_____

_____

_____

How did this message speak to your heart?

_____

_____

_____

_____

ENJOYING COMPANY

A message delivered to the men at Transformation Ranch on December 28, 2019.

The Message

Battles we all endure. My battles and your battles aren't the same, but the Jesus who fights for us is. Jesus enjoys seeing you enjoy each other today. Many individuals aren't as fortunate to enjoy other people's company. Many individuals are completely alone tonight. But even though you may think you're alone because your loved ones aren't here, you're not! Enjoy this time Jesus has blessed each of you with. Enjoy striving to let these men be family during difficult seasons such as this.

Battles teach us to trust completely in Jesus for everything. Could you all forgive me because I'm not myself tonight? But it is important to me to encourage each of you no matter how I feel.

Jesus loves all of you!

The Scriptures

> Have not I commanded thee? Be strong and of a good courage; be not afraid, neither be thou dismayed: for the Lord thy God is with thee whithersoever thou goest. (Joshua 1:9)

> The Lord shall fight for you, and ye shall hold your peace. (Exodus 14:14)

> Wherefore comfort yourselves together, and edify one another, even as also ye do. (1 Thessalonians 5:11)

THE REFLECTION

Could a light be brighter if people combined all their lights for them to shine as one? Of course it could! Call on the Lord to help fight for you. Brothers, each one of you are called to encourage each other. Can you be the answer to someone's call for help?

_____

_____

_____

_____

_____

Battle not alone. Talk to God about your concerns. Can all my brothers faint not? Brothers, please comfort each other. Whom can you comfort today?

_____

_____

_____

_____

_____

How did this message speak to your heart?

_____

_____

_____

_____

_____

COMPLETE SURRENDER

A message delivered to the men at Transformation Ranch at Tombigbee State Park Retreat on February 29, 2020.

The Message

Black days have surrounded me most of this week. Pain has caused me to desire Heaven more than ever before, but Jesus informed me that He is not done with me. And He informed me that He is not done with you. He is constantly doing new things in us. He is truly the Potter, and we are His clay. Believe me, I am under constant attack from enemies because I'm Jesus's child. I know I haven't done many of the things that some of you have chosen to do, but I know what it's like to suffer each day. Jesus is your hope. Jesus delights in each of you. You know what choices you made. Believe me, He tells me often how much He loves His children. Just trust me if you think otherwise.

Turn everything over to Jesus, and He will use your life to glorify God. For today and the rest of your time here, enjoy only listening for Jesus. Tune out this world. Let Jesus have complete control of your mind, and enemies will flee. One of my reasons for Jesus leaving me here for now is to help guys just like you understand that they can be free in Christ even though bound in prison. I'm diligently working on a devotional to guide men to know Jesus like never before and to challenge your thoughts about where you are in Christ. I'll pray for each one of you.

The Scriptures

> Remember ye not the former things, neither consider the things of old. Behold, I will do a new thing; now it shall spring forth; shall ye not know it? I will even make a way in the wilderness, and rivers in the desert. (Isaiah 43:18–19)

> But now, O Lord, Thou art our Father; we are the clay, and Thou our Potter; and we all are the work of Thy hand. (Isaiah 64:8)

> He brought me forth also into a large place; He delivered me, because He delighted in me. (Psalm 18:19)

THE REFLECTION

Shoes help provide great comfort for our feet, but coating our minds with truth from God's Word provides comfort for our souls. My desire is that each of you enjoy getting your comfort from Jesus instead of things that don't last! Make a list of the things that could be replaced with Jesus.

_____

_____

_____

_____

Many of you still hunger for instant gratification. Getting fed from God's Word is comfort that never ceases. Prayer marks us as being healed of hunger if our faith is in God's comforting truths. Take time to seek comfort in God through His scriptures and prayer. Write the scripture that you found to comfort your soul.

_____

_____

_____

_____

How did this message speak to your heart?

_____

_____

_____

_____

AMAZING GRACE[6]

Amazing grace, how sweet the sound that saved a wretch like me.
We once were lost, but now we are found; we were blind, but now we see.

'Twas Jesus's comfort that comforted us, and Jesus's comfort we need.
How precious did all the Christians feel, the hour they believed.

As for me and every Christian, church isn't about a show.
Only Jesus is our constant joy, but do you truly know?

Fall on your face in awe of God for He holds eternity.
Beneath our cuts and wounded hearts, enough of God you'll see!

God gets us through our toughest days, and He loves being with you.
Calling out to Him is always wise
as He's longing to carry you through.

Feeling happy each day is hard, but give it over to God!
Bring all your troubles and lay them down, find peace salvation awed.[7]

Before Christians desired Jesus, Jesus desired us first.
Begin today asking God to
know how to be used on this earth!

(Adapted by Caleb Brian Rodgers, completed on February 9, 2017.)

---

[6] "Amazing Grace" was rewritten by Caleb during some of his most painful days.
[7] This means salvation brings peace to our lives and a feeling of awe only salvation creates.

PLAN OF SALVATION

(Published in his book *Hope in Jesus*.)

The Message

Follow along with me please after you know without a doubt that you are ready to turn from your way of living and let Jesus show you His idea for living!

Jesus is the Son of God!

God sent Jesus to Earth in the form of a man to save all of us. People all over the Earth put God last, but God wants us to put Him first! God especially loves each individual reading this message. Following Jesus's steps after you decide to accept Him into your heart is the best decision you'll ever make. Please pray this prayer with me today to begin serving our Jesus:

> Dear God,
>
> I am sorry for my mistakes. Would you forgive me? Help me to obey You. I run away from my sins now only to run to You!
>
> I'm now ready to accept Jesus into my heart. My heart belongs to You.
>
> Thank You, God, and enjoy using my life to serve You! I'm praying this with Jesus now in my heart. Amen!

NOTES

Thank you for pouring out your heart in this devotional journal. Feel free to share with me how Jesus removed your chains and set you free.

Caleb

Mail: Just Jesus Inc, PO Box 222, Tupelo, MS 38802-0222

Email: befreeinchrist2020@gmail.com
justJesusinc2020@gmail.com

Facebook: Be Free in Christ: A Road Map to Freedom for Men (or personal facebook page @ Caleb Rodgers Updates)

If you would like to make a donation to help distribute these books to men in various programs worldwide, please visit www.JustJesusInc.com.

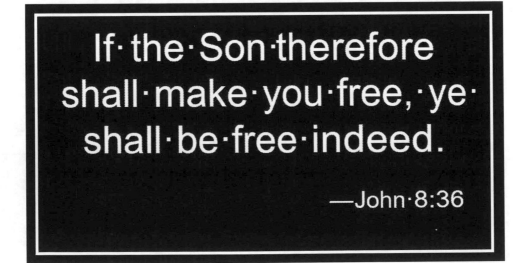

If·the·Son·therefore shall·make·you·free,·ye· shall·be·free·indeed.

—John·8:36

Printed in the United States
by Baker & Taylor Publisher Services